THE
ROSE AND CROWN

A Play in One Act

by

J. B. PRIESTLEY

SAMUEL FRENCH

LONDON
NEW YORK   SYDNEY   TORONTO   HOLLYWOOD

FOR AMATEUR PRODUCTION ENQUIRIES

UNITED KINGDOM AND WORLD
EXCLUDING NORTH AMERICA
plays@samuelfrench.co.uk
020 7255 4302/01

Each title is subject to availability from Samuel French, depending upon country of performance.

CHARACTERS

Mr. Stone.
Mrs. Reed.
Percy Randle.
Ivy Randle.
Ma Peck.
Harry Tully.
A Stranger.

The action takes place in the Public Bar of the " Rose and Crown," a small public house in North-East London. The time is an early evening in early autumn.

THE ROSE AND CROWN

The SCENE *is the Public Bar of a small public house in a poorish district of North-East London.*

If an actual set is used, it should show a dingy and rather cheerless room, with perhaps one curtained window and the usual advertisements, preferably faded in colour, on the walls. The door is C. *up stage, and so long as it is practicable it can either be a simple single door or the familiar swing doors. The actual bar is not seen, being on the fourth wall. What is seen, just inside the setting line, is the counter of the bar, cut through the middle, so to speak, and quite solidly built. (See the Ground Plan.) It should be about 12 feet wide. As no landlord can be seen—though the actors have to play, very carefully, as if he were there—the business of receiving drinks and paying for them must be imaginary business; but, if the producer prefers the actors to have glasses in their hands—and this is better—then the bar counter must be built fairly solidly to the ground, and these glasses must be produced cunningly by the actors from shelves, invisible to the audience, fastened on to the upstage side of the bar.*

But for a simple production no actual set is necessary, only the door at back and the bar counter, with drab curtains as walls.

The lighting is fairly strong but should have a dreary effect. It is absolutely essential that there should be at least one strong F.O.H. spot. Ideally, the play should be lit from the front.

At the rise of the CURTAIN, *the stage is empty for a moment, and then* STONE *enters. He is a grumpy middle-aged man, fattish, shabby, but not too shabby. He can smoke an unpleasant little pipe. He carries an evening paper. Like the others who follow, he must go through the pantomime of ordering the drink, etc. very carefully, and it is primarily his business to create the illusion of the invisible landlord, FRED, who is presumed to enter each time, below the bar, from R.*

STONE (*grumpily, at the counter somewhat R. of C., as he follows "FRED" with his eyes from L. to C.*). . . . And good evening to you, Fred, if you want to call it a good evening . . . Pint of brown . . . (*He glances at his paper, then goes through the business of receiving and paying for his drink, then taking a pull at it. He looks suspiciously at his paper again.*) What? No, I 'aven't seen Charlie lately, and I don't know that I want to . . . well, 'e doesn't amuse *me* . . . (*Looking up.*) All right, Fred, it takes all sorts to make a world. I wish some of 'em 'ud make me a few two-inch lead pipes . . . No, not for love nor money. Drive yer barmy. (*He has now settled down, staring gloomily down at his paper, having moved towards the R.C. corner of the bar.*) Two planes crash. I'm not surprised. There'll be plenty more before so long, you'll see. Cars too. You watch it. Just blue murder, that's all—blue murder. No proper precautions—that's the trouble —no proper precautions . . . (*He half listens as* FRED *apparently tries to tell him a story, then interrupts.*) If it's the one about the bookie who stayed with the widow at Doncaster I've 'eard it. (*He stares at his paper again.*)

(MRS. REED *now enters. She is a thin middle-aged woman, loquacious and mournful.*)

MRS. REED (*moving down* C., *to the bar*). Good evenin', Fred. Good evenin', Mr. Stone.
STONE (*shortly*). Evenin'.

Mrs. Reed (*to the landlord*). I'll take a drop o' stout, Fred—Guinness if you 'ave it. I feel that tired some o' these nights—properly worn-out, you might say—that I don't feel like eatin' nothing—an' only a nice drop o' stout will sit on my stomach. I went out to my sister's last night—the one that's married to a painter an' decorator with a nice business of 'is own—at least it *was* a nice business once—an' she give us rissoles—an' nice an' tasty they seemed at the time—but when I got 'ome my inside felt 'eavy as lead an' burnin' like fire——

(*She has now gone through the business of receiving and paying for her drink. Her story is broken off because* Stone *stares disapprovingly at her and makes a tut-tutting sound. She stares aggressively at him now.*)

'Ow d'you mean—t-t-t-t?

Stone (*heavily*). I mean I've got enough troubles of me own, Mrs. Reed—without you servin' up your rissoles an' your inside——

Mrs. Reed (*on her dignity*). Oh—well, if it comes to that, Mr. Stone—I've got plenty o' troubles of *my* own—an' one of 'em is that you won't come an' put a new pipe in my sink——

Stone (*indignantly*). If I've told you once, Mrs. Reed, I've told you a dozen times—I can't put a new pipe in till I *get* a new pipe. That stands to reason, doesn't it?

Mrs. Reed (*very dubiously*). Does it?

Stone (*exasperated*). Look—I spend all day tryin' to argue with people like you——

Mrs. Reed. Not with me, you don't. I've something better to do——

Stone. I said "People *like* you." An' when I can take 'alf an hour off of an evening, like this, I want to give it all a rest, see? But I can't put a new pipe in for you if I 'aven't got a new pipe to put in, can I? Is that reasonable—or isn't it?

MRS. REED (*darkly*). I don't know. What I *do* know is that Mrs. Ferguson, three doors down, 'as 'ad a whole bathroom put in—double-yew and all——

STONE. Well, I don't know anything about that —she isn't a customer of mine——

MRS. REED. No, that's easy to see. Black Market, I expect. It all goes together. 'Aving her 'air waved every five minutes an' nippin' into the Saloon Bar of the White Horse for gins an' limes—I've 'eard about 'er——

STONE (*grumpily, trying to read*). Well, I 'aven't, an' I don't want to. (*He reads.*)

(MRS. REED *stares at him indignantly, and then looks bored. It is obvious that the landlord is no longer in this bar.* MRS. REED *tries again.*)

MRS. REED (*moving a little towards* R.C.). 'Ave you read where it says that woman in Molesley Terrace gassed herself 'cos 'er 'usband went an' sold the pianner to go bettin' at the dogs?

(STONE *merely grunts, without looking at her. After another moment, during which* MRS. REED *gives up any attempt to interest* STONE, PERCY *and* IVY RANDLE *enter. They are a young married couple. He is tallish, thin, pessimistic. She is small and slight, fearful and rather wistful. They come down to the bar on the* L. *of* MRS. REED, *who looks at them with interest, and then calls officiously for the landlord.*)

Fred—Fred!

(*We see* "FRED" *enter by the answering stares of* MRS. REED *and the* RANDLES.)

PERCY (*as if replying to* "FRED"). No, I don't think it *is* a very nice night.

IVY (*in a tiny voice*). It's turned quite cold.

PERCY (*who is* L. *of* IVY). What yer 'avin', Ivy? Bitter or mild?

Ivy. Mild, I think, Percy.

Percy. 'Alf of bitter, 'alf of mild. (*He goes through business of getting drinks and paying.*)

(Ivy *and* Mrs. Reed *exchange tentative mournful smiles.*)

Well here you are, Ivy. Now drink it, don't sip it.

Ivy (*to* Mrs. Reed). He always says that to me, an' I know I never do drink it—I always sip it. I don't think I like beer really—I just come in to keep Percy company—what I really enjoy is a nice glass of port wine.

Percy (*with sad raillery*). You an' your port wine! (*He moves to the* L.C. *corner of the bar.*)

Mrs. Reed. I used to like a small port now and then meself—but now, look at the price, even when you can get it.

Ivy. That's right.

Percy. Isn't much of it about these days.

Stone (*heavily*). There's plenty o' port wine about, if you keep your eyes open——

Mrs. Reed (*aggressively*). Oh—is there? News to me.

Percy. Same 'ere.

Stone. Well, there is—only it's muck. Like a lot of other things now—it's muck. (*He returns to his paper.*)

Mrs. Reed (*to* Ivy). 'Aven't I seen you at Magby's—the greengrocer's at the corner?

Ivy. I expect you 'ave. Though I've only just started going there.

Mrs. Reed (*gloomily*). You want to watch 'im.

Percy. Isn't that just what I said, Ivy?

Ivy. Yes, you did, Percy. (*To* Mrs. Reed.) My 'usband said just the same thing. "You'll 'ave to watch 'im," he said.

Mrs. Reed. He doesn't try it on with me any more—he knows better.

Stone (*looking up, aggressively*). Try what on?

MRS. REED. Never you mind. I'm not talking to you, Mr. Stone. (*To* IVY.) But you watch 'im.

STONE (*heavily*). 'Ave you people ever 'eard of the lor of slander?

MRS. REED. Go on. Nobody's gettin' slandered.

IVY (*alarmed*). Oo—I never said anything, did I? Did I, Percy? (*She moves a little towards* PERCY.)

STONE. I didn't say you did. But *she* did. And *'e* did. An' what I say is that there's such a thing as the lor of slander. I'm a tradesman an' shopkeeper meself——

MRS. REED. That's right—an' you're all in a click, if you ask me.

PERCY (*gloomily*). I wouldn't be surprised.

IVY (*in a frightened whisper*). Shut up, Percy.

PERCY. Why should I?

MRS. REED. Don't you. (*She moves to a little L. of C., nearer* IVY.)

PERCY. This—er—gentleman 'ere says 'e's a tradesman an' shopkeeper. Well, I an' my wife are customers, that's what I say. That used to be something, one time, to be a customer.

MRS. REED. Yes, when they couldn't afford to treat you like dirt.

STONE (*rather violently*). Nobody wants to treat anybody like dirt except when they behave like dirt——

MRS. REED (*angrily*). Who behaves like dirt? (*She moves to C. as she continues.*) That's casting aspertions, that is, an' it's personal an' not called for. Dirt indeed! If you'd attend to my sink like I've asked you to do——

STONE (*cutting in*). There it goes again. That's just what I mean. Customers! They won't listen to reason, just won't listen to reason. I suppose you think I can grow new lead pipes in the back garden like sticks of flamin' rhubarb!

IVY (*hopefully*). I can't touch rhubarb. Never could.

STONE (*in despair*). Am I askin' you to touch rhubarb?

PERCY. That's right. You're off the argument there, Ivy. It's like I told you. You will get off the argument.

MRS. REED. Well, who wants to get on to the argument? Argument! Argument! There's too much argument nowadays.

IVY. That's what I keep tellin' Percy.

(STONE *wags his head angrily and makes a loud tut-tutting sound, then retires to his paper.* MRS. REED *makes a face at him, for* IVY'S *benefit.* IVY *giggles and tries to suppress it.* PERCY *looks at her severely.*)

MRS. REED (*returning towards* IVY). I'm like that about tomatoes.

IVY. Are you reelly?

MRS. REED. It come over me quite sudden too. One day, you might say, I properly enjoyed a tomato. Next day, as you might say, I couldn't face one. An' I been like that ever since. But I've 'ad a lot of trouble with my inside—delicate.

IVY. My 'usband's sister's just the same. Isn't she, Percy?

PERCY (L. *of the* L.C. *corner of the bar*). Been like it ever since she was a kiddie, Doris has. An' it doesn't make for 'appiness, does it?

MRS. REED. 'Appiness? Don't make me laugh. Look—I wouldn't know it if I saw it now.

STONE. Don't worry. You won't see it.

MRS. REED (*ignoring him*). I'll tell you straight —what with one thing an' another—if I was asked right out if life was worth living—d'you know what I'd say? I'd say No. Honestly I would.

IVY. Percy says the same thing sometimes. (*Turning to* PERCY.) Don't you, Percy?

PERCY. Now an' again. I'm not like some chaps —I notice things an' try an' think a bit. And then

—as Ivy says—it gets me down. Yes, I'll admit it. It gets me down.

STONE (*grimly*). If it gets you down now, what are you going to be like at my age? You 'aven't 'ardly started yet. You wait!

PERCY. It may be as bad for me as it is for you. There needn't be any waiting about it.

STONE (*grimmer still*). You'll see. (*He moves a pace or two in, to* R.C.) Just wait till you 'ave to try an' run a business with everybody screamin' at you—an' you've got a family that's grabbin' everything you earn—an' your 'air's fallin' out an' your teeth's droppin' out—an' you get varicose veins an' lumbago——

IVY (*proudly*). Percy has very responsible work at the warehouse—an' he has to 'elp to keep 'is mother—an' he gets terrible 'eadaches. Don't you, Percy?

PERCY. Cruel. That's the only word for 'em. Cruel. An' there's no cure. 'Ad 'em all me life.

MRS. REED (*sighing*). Oh—well—if it isn't one thing it's always another.

IVY. That's right. Though I suppose it's a long road that 'as no turning.

STONE. Well, what if it is? Where does that get you?

PERCY (*with dignity*). My wife was just passin' a remark, that's all. No need to pick on 'er like that.

MRS. REED. Take no notice of 'im. Got out of the wrong side of the bed this morning.

STONE. 'Ow do you know?

MRS. REED (*turning to face* STONE). That's personal an' uncalled for again, if you ask me.

PERCY. Quite so. Ungentlemanly.

STONE (*disgusted*). Oh—turn it up.

(*He turns away* R., *and stares at his paper. The others relapse into a gloomy silence.* MA PECK *now enters. She is an untidy old woman who looks*

a bitter and disreputable character. Mrs. Reed
sees her as she advances slowly down c.)

Mrs. Reed (*to nobody in particular*). I understood
Fred Norton 'ere was tryin' to keep a respectable
house.

Ma Peck (*arriving at the bar on the* r. *of* Mrs.
Reed). Did you pass a remark to me, Mrs. What's-it?

Mrs. Reed (*to* Ma Peck; *with dignity*). No, I
didn't. Not to you. I was speakin' to this lady 'ere.

Ma Peck (*with mock refinement*). Oh—to this
lady 'ere—was you? Charming weather we're 'aving
—except that the nights is drawin' in rather. Grrrr!
(*She bangs on the bar counter, and shouts.*) Hoy
—what's your name! Fred! (*She goes through
business of watching him enter the bar, and grins.*)
Now then—just look after an old woman who's 'ad
more than 'er share of trouble. I want a glass of
brown with a nice drop o' gin in it . . . Go on,
of course you've some gin . . . Don't worry, you
won't see too much of me this time, 'cos I can only
afford one go, an' I don't see any o' this lot paying
for a few more for me.

Mrs. Reed. The last time anybody did, you was
'ad up in Court.

Stone (*nastily, without looking up from his paper*).
And not for the first time neither.

Ma Peck. Well, they'll never 'ave you for bein'
drunk an' disorderly. You're too mean—even to
yerself. Stone by name, an' Stone by nature. And
yer father was just the same.

Stone (*looking up and moving a pace in, to* r.c.).
Now—look 'ere——

(*But it is obvious that the landlord has protested too,
and* Ma *listens and replies to him, having now got
her drink.*)

Ma Peck (*to the landlord*). All right, Fred boy
Not another word, I promise. I'll be good.

(*She drinks, and obviously enjoys her drink, while*
    STONE *returns* R., *and takes up his paper.*)

I'm only a daft old woman that's buried everybody
that ever cared anything for her—an' with one foot
in the grave. (*Moving round, above* MRS. REED, *to
the shrinking* IVY.) You'll come to it, dearie, if you
live long enough—you'll come to it.

(*They are silent and look glum.* MA PECK *glances
    from one to the other.*)

'Ere, I come in 'ere to be cheered up a bit. What's
the matter with you lot? You're young an' got yer
'ealth an' strength, 'aven't yer?
    PERCY (*with dignity*). We've got our troubles
same as you. In fact, we was just talking about 'em.
    IVY (*warning him*). Percy!

(IVY *and* PERCY *shift a little* L., *along the bar.*)

    MA PECK (L. *of* MRS. REED). Percy! So Percy's
got 'is little troubles, 'as 'e? Poor Percy!
    PERCY. All right, Ma. Not so much of it.
    MA PECK. Ma! Listen, Percy, I've buried five
men—two 'usbands an' three sons—that would 'ave
eaten you for breakfast—yes, an' then asked for some
'addock. (*Returning to* C.) Ask Mr. Stone there—
'e knows. (*She looks at* STONE, *who keeps his eyes
on his paper.*) Well, what's in the paper?
    STONE (*growling*). A lot o' dam' bad news, as
usual.
    MA PECK. I dare say. But it's my bad news that
worries me—not theirs. (*Speaking across to* IVY.)
What do you say, ducks?
    IVY. Yes, that's right.
    MA PECK. That's right, is it? Well, I'll bet you
don't 'ave much trouble with Percy 'ere—unless 'e
doesn't always wipe 'is nice little shoes clean when
'e comes in. When I was your age, dearie, I was
married to a sergeant in the Marines, an' when 'e

came 'ome—something 'appened—one way or the other—upstairs or down—an' you knew you'd got a man in the 'ouse. (*She sprawls mournfully on the bar at* c., *almost talking to herself.*) Oh—Gawd—what's the use o' talkin'? Nobody knows any more, an' nobody cares. An' why the 'ell should they? Old Ma Peck! She ought to be quietly pushing the daisies up somewhere like the rest o' the Pecks. (*She turns to the others.*) You an' your troubles! Just wait till you're old an' alone an' nobody wants you any more—an' you're awake night after night—an' every bone in your rotten old carcase is aching! (*Almost mumbling to herself.*) An' then when you come in to enjoy a drink an' some lively company —same as there used to be—you find nothin' but a handful o' long-faced, scowling bloody dummies. Oh —Gawd's bitter truth—but I wish I was dead an' done with it.

(*There is a gloomy silence. This is broken by the entrance, brisk and hearty, of* HARRY TULLY. *He is any age between thirty-five and fifty, decently though not well dressed, and a healthy, jovial, matey fellow.*)

HARRY (*coming down* R. *of* MA PECK). Evening, everybody! Thickening a bit outside tonight, but a nice smell of autumn about it. Always reminds me of when I was a lad. Don't know why, but it does. Good-evening, Mr. Stone. How's business?

STONE. Evening. An' business is the same as usual these days—rotten!

HARRY. Go on! You're not doing so bad. I know. (*Crossing above* MA PECK *to her* L.) How are you, Mrs. Reed?

MRS. REED. About the same. It's my inside.

HARRY (*between* MA PECK *and* MRS. REED). Hard luck. But you're looking better. Now where's Fred? (*He leans across and looks towards the un-seen door* L.)

MA PECK (*suddenly looking up*). I know you—Harry Tully.

HARRY (*turning to* MA PECK). That's right. And I know you, Ma. Enjoying yourself?

MA PECK (*shifting a little* R.C.). Miserable as hell, Harry, boy. This lot act as if they'd be better dead, an' I feel it.

HARRY. Well, have one with me, Ma.

MA PECK. That's a good boy. Now, don't go, Harry.

HARRY. I'm not going, I've only just arrived. Pull yourself together, Ma. Then you can tell me some of them funny stories that Mr. Stone's been telling you.

MA PECK. What—'*im*? If he had a funny story, he wouldn't part with it. This is Percy, Harry.

HARRY (*moving around* MRS. REED *to the* RANDLES). How are you, Percy? This the wife?

IVY (*shyly*). Yes.

HARRY. Pleased to meet you. Hoy, Fred! Don't keep the customers waiting. (*He obviously sees* "FRED" *enter, and moves back to* C.) How's it going, Fred? . . . That's right. It might be better, but it might easily be a hundred times worse. Remember that night we all jumped for it under the bar counter? And the night we pulled Meaty an' his missis an' the kids out of the back of the shop? It's Bob's your uncle now compared with them days. Well, a pint of half-and-half for me, Fred, and a small brown with a drop of gin for Ma here . . . Go on, Fred, you can find a drop for old Ma . . . That's right, Fred. Oh—and what about Mrs. Percy here—one for the bride, eh? All right to you, eh, Percy?

PERCY. Oh—certainly. What would you like, Ivy?

IVY (*shyly*). There isn't any port wine, is there —just a little glass?

HARRY. Yes, every time. Fred's got some port

wine somewhere, haven't you, Fred . . . Right you are, then. In a minute we'll settle down and make our miserable souls happy. Eh, Ma?

MA PECK. You're a good boy, Harry.

HARRY. Don't you believe it. (*To* MRS. REED.) What do you say, Mrs. Reed? You've heard a thing or two about me, haven't you?

STONE (*grimly*). If she hasn't, *I* have.

MA PECK. Nobody ever believed a plumber yet, and we're not going to start now.

HARRY. O-ho! Well, it served you right for talking out of turn. Good old Ma! Now, here we are. Thanks, Fred. (*He goes through the pantomime of taking the drinks, paying for them, handing one to* MA *and carrying another to* IVY, *then returning* C. *to his own drink and addressing the landlord.*) All right, Fred. You pop off. I know you're busy in the other bar.

(*They watch "* FRED *" go, then* HARRY *holds up his glass, and* MA *and* IVY *hold up theirs.*)

MA PECK. All the best, Harry boy!

HARRY. And to you, Ma.

IVY (*shyly*). All the best!

HARRY (*speaking across to* IVY, *very heartily*). Same to you, my dear, and may we all live a hundred years.

(*As they drink, the* STRANGER *enters quietly. He is not extraordinary and yet not quite ordinary. He is a plumpish middle-aged man with a rather pale clean-shaven face, dressed in dark clothes. The others ignore him, and he remains in the background for the moment.*)

STONE. What for?

HARRY. How do you mean—what for?

STONE. I mean—why do you want to live a hundred years?

HARRY. Oh—I see. Just a saying, that's all.

Still, it 'ud be all right to me. To enjoy life, y'know——

MA PECK. Don't talk to this lot about enjoying life. They wouldn't know what you mean.

MRS. REED (*leaning over the bar and speaking across to* MA PECK). Well, just before he came in, you were carrying on—as if you wished you was dead.

MA PECK. Well, so I did, and so would you in my place. As for you, you're dead already, only you don't know it.

HARRY (*at* C. *a pace above the bar*). Now, Ma, Mrs. Reed's all right in her own way, and we're all friends here. I must tell you, I had a good laugh today——

STONE (*cutting in, almost angrily*). Just a minute, Harry Tully. Before you start on the good laugh, I want you to answer just one question for my benefit.

HARRY (*cheerfully*). Go on. I'll buy it.

STONE. What have *you* got to be so cheerful about?

HARRY (*taking a pace to the bar, and speaking across to* STONE). Well, what have you got to be so miserable about?

STONE. Do you want me to tell you?

HARRY. No, I've heard it before. (*He drinks.*)

STONE (*almost angry again*). You're no better off than the rest of us. You're in the same old mess-up we're all in. If you're doing as well as I'm doing, I'd be surprised——

HARRY. So would I.

STONE. Well, what's the idea then?

PERCY (*leaning over the* L. *angled section of the bar*). If you ask me—and I read a piece about it in a magazine—it's something to do with glands——

IVY (*shocked*). Percy, don't be rude.

PERCY. It's not rude—it's scientific. Glands.

HARRY. Can't say. I don't read magazines. But what I say is this—we're alive and kicking, aren't we? All right then.

PERCY. Yes, but where does that get you?

STONE. Nowhere. He doesn't know what he's talking about.

STRANGER (*politely, advancing to down* L.C.). Excuse me!

(*He has a quiet, apologetic, but curiously authoritative tone. They all turn and stare at him.*)

STONE. What's the matter?

STRANGER. You must excuse me for interrupting you, but I'm here on business, you know, and I'm afraid I'll have to get on with it, if you don't mind.

HARRY. Well, we're not stopping you. Do you want to see the landlord—Fred?

STRANGER. Oh—no, that's not necessary. (*Coming down to the bar between* HARRY *and* MRS. REED.) One of you will do very well. In fact it'll have to be one of you.

STONE. Look here, if you're trying to sell us something, you can leave me out now. I've been had before.

STRANGER. No, no. I'm not trying to sell you anything. (*He looks at them for a moment.*)

(IVY *clutches her husband's arm.*)

IVY (*in a whisper*). Percy—I'm frightened.

PERCY (*who is not so sure*). It's all right, Ivy. (*With all his courage, staring at the* STRANGER.) 'Ere —what's the idea? Nobody asked you to come in 'ere.

STRANGER. Quite so. But, don't forget, this is a public house.

HARRY (*who has withdrawn a pace up stage, his eyes on the* STRANGER). Certainly. Got as much right here as we have. But if you've got anything to say, I think I'd get on with it, chum.

STRANGER (*turning to* HARRY). That's what I said myself, if you remember, when I apologized for interrupting you. And now I'll explain——

Mrs. Reed (*cutting in, sharply*). You needn't do any explaining to me.

(*The* Stranger *turns to her.*)

I don't see why you should come botherin' us—it isn't supposed to be allowed in most bars—an' I'm going to 'ave a word with the landlord, Fred Norton.

Stranger (*still apologetically*). I'm afraid you can't now. We shall have to get our little bit of business done before Fred can come in again.

Mrs. Reed. Don't be silly. 'Ave 'im 'ere in a tick. (*She raps on the counter and turns to call* Fred. *The call dies in her throat as she stares in amazement. She points to where we have imagined* Fred *to enter from the other bar down* L., *below the bar.*) Look—it's all walled up—or something——

(*The others stare in amazement, and then* Ivy *gives a frightened scream.*)

Ivy. It's a marble slab—like a cemetery——
(*She turns to cling to* Percy, *who has moved on her* L.)

Stone (*who is the farthest away below the* R.C. *corner of the bar*). Go on—it can't be.

Harry (*quietly*). It is, though.

(*They all turn now slowly, and stare at the* Stranger, *who looks at them with a little apologetic smile.*)

Ma Peck. I knew you was a rum sort o' sausage from the start.

Stranger. Now, Ma Peck——

Ma Peck (*cutting in; sharply*). Who give yer my name?

Stranger. I know all your names. I have to—in my business. (*He points to each one as he recites their names.*) Edward Stone. Harry Tully. Percy Randle. Ivy Randle. Bertha Reed. Kathleen Peck —commonly known as Ma Peck. All right, eh?

Ivy (*urgently*). Percy, let's go.

PERCY. Hold on a minute, then we'll go.

STRANGER (*smiling apologetically*). You can't go until I've finished.

STONE (*straightening up, as if about to go*). I'll go when I like.

STRANGER. I don't think so.

(STONE *checks, and stares at the* STRANGER.)

MA PECK. He's a busy—a 'tec—that's what 'e is.

HARRY (*who is still a pace above the bar*). No, he isn't. (*To the* STRANGER*; coming close to the bar.*) Well, tell us what it's all about.

STRANGER. Quite simple, really. Every day people die, don't they? Not the same number every day, of course, but we have to keep up a certain average. No doubt you've wondered how it's done—who picks out the ones who are going to die. Now, it's all right saying "Death went to that house" or "Death struck down this man," but of course it's obvious Death couldn't do it all by himself. There's got to be some sort of organization—I'm the representative for the Number Two North-Eastern District of London—— (*He produces a large black-edged card or two and hands them to the others, who stare at them and pass them on, then stare at him in wondering silence. He continues smoothly, still in an easy and rather apologetic strain.*) Now, my quota for today was eleven, for my district, and I worked off eight early this morning, which is the best time of course, and then I chose two more this afternoon—but I had some trouble about a little boy—nice kid just turned four —and I got a bit mixed up and thought I'd finished for the day. So I was on my way home when I suddenly remembered I was one short of my quota, so I looked in here. Of course I could have picked out one of you, in the usual way, but I thought it would make a nice change and that you'd appreciate it for once if I let you decide which one of you it should be.

Ivy (*gasping*). To die—tonight——?

STRANGER (*smoothly*). That's it. Don't forget, you've all got to die sometime. It isn't as if some died and some didn't—that would be a horrible idea. As it is, it's only a matter of one of you obliging the rest of you, and me, by taking an earlier turn.

STONE. I don't believe a word of it, but I've 'eard quite enough—and I'm going. (*He adjusts his hat and buttons his jacket, defiantly.*)

STRANGER. I told you—nobody can go now until I've finished.

STONE (*gripping the counter and leaning forward*). You try an' stop me.

STRANGER. Well, you try and go. After all, you can't do a job like this without having a bit of authority. And nobody can say I haven't been trying to make it all easy and pleasant for everybody. I had to block up that bar, of course, because we have to settle it among ourselves without being interrupted.

STONE (*pointing to the door up* C.). That door isn't blocked up, and now I'm going straight through it. (*He marches towards the door, then suddenly stops and cries out with pain, twisting and wriggling with it.*)

(MA PECK *and* HARRY *have backed one pace up* R. *so that this can be seen by the audience.*)

(*Groaning.*) It's this damned back o' mine. Can't move a step farther.

STRANGER (*moving a pace up stage of the bar*). It hits you where you're weakest. We know, of course. (*Turning to the others.*) Now, anybody else like to try—so as not to waste much more time?

(STONE *sullenly returns to his place at* R.)

MRS. REED (*shivering and desperate*). Yes, I'm going.

STRANGER (*coolly*). It'll get you in the stomach, I imagine. Just try—and see.

(MRS. REED *runs for it to up* C., *but within three or four paces of the door is stopped as if by a blow at her stomach, and she too cries out in pain and bends almost double. Care must be taken not to overplay this little scene.*)

MA PECK (*muttering, coming down a pace*). Hell's Judas!—but if he isn't the devil 'imself—he's tellin' us nothin' less than the truth.

(STONE *is now shakily finishing his drink.* MRS. REED, *softly whimpering, comes back to her place* L.C. *All stare wonderingly at the* STRANGER.)

STRANGER (*at* C., *still slightly above the bar, looking at them,* R. *and* L.). Well, that's that. And now the question is—which one is it to be?

STONE. All right, that's easy. (*He points dramatically at* MA PECK, *who has turned to him.*)

MA PECK (*aghast*). What—me? (*She withdraws a pace up stage, level with* HARRY.)

STONE. Yes, you. (*He speaks eagerly across to the* STRANGER.) Just before you come in—an' just before Harry Tully 'ere stood 'er another drink—she was complainin' an' moanin' about being old an' alone an' saying she wished she was dead an' done with it——

PERCY. That's right. I heard her.

MA PECK (*indignantly*). There you are—pick on a poor old woman who's never done nobody any 'arm an' just because she 'asn't the price of another drink just talks daft for a minute——

MRS. REED (*cutting in*). But we all 'eard you—sayin' you'd nobody left an' you ought to be pushin' the daisies up——

MA PECK (*furiously cutting in*). Go on, you! (*She comes to the bar, grips it, and speaks across.*) That's just my silly talk—but what about you, eh? Always goin' on about your terrible inside—an' never gettin' a bit o' pleasure out of anything. What 'ave you got to live for, I'd like to know?

Mrs. Reed (*angrily*). I'm twenty-five years younger than you—an' you said yerself you'd one foot in the grave——

Ma Peck. Yes, but the other foot's alive all right —an' for two pins I'd use it to kick——

Harry (*coming down a pace to her*). Now, now, Ma—that's no way to carry on. (*Patting her shoulder.*) Let's take it easy.

Ma Peck (*almost tearfully*). All right, Harry, you're a good boy. But don't let 'em put it on me —a poor old woman who 'asn't seen a priest nor the inside of a church for thirty years—and isn't fit to die yet. (*To the* Stranger.) It's got to be tonight, 'asn't it?

Stranger (*prominently looking at his watch*). **Yes**, and soon too. I can't give you more than another quarter of an hour. He'll be here then for one of you.

Percy (*uneasily*). Who's he?

Stranger. We needn't go into that. One of my superiors. It's a big organization. (*Until he speaks again, he remains withdrawn, a pace above the bar.*)

Percy (*uneasily*). I see. Well——

Ivy (*urgently*). Percy—don't interfere.

Percy. I was only goin' to say it's got to be one of them three. (*He indicates* Ma Peck, Mrs. Reed *and* Stone.)

Mrs. Reed. Oh—'as it—what's the matter with *you*?

Stone. Just what I was goin' to say. Who told us life wasn't worth living?

Percy (*hastily*). She did—Mrs. Reed. She said if she was asked right out, she would say No—it wasn't worth living——

Mrs. Reed (*cutting in*). And then your wife said that was what you was always saying——

Ivy (*desperately*). I didn't say *always*—I only said *sometimes*—honestly I did.

Stone. He said it got 'im down. We 'eard 'im.

Ivy (*desperately*). It's only 'is way of talking. I

know 'im. An' he's young—an' we've only just got married—an' got a nice little 'ome together——

STONE. He doesn't seem to be enjoying it much.

IVY. He does—he loves it really—it's only his way of talkin'. (*Then, with the sudden boldness of the shy.*) You talked a lot worse than he did—tellin' us just to wait until we got older——

STONE. That's just a manner of speakin'. I've got a business. I've got responsibilities. It'll make a lot o' difference to people if I suddenly pop off. What does it matter to one of you youngsters? Save yourselves a lot o' worry.

PERCY. Well, you can save yourself some now, can't you?

STONE. Talk sense.

MRS. REED. Well, 'e is talkin' sense. You was easily the worst of the lot, Ted Stone, grumble, grumble, grumble——

STONE (*almost shouting*). All right, I grumble. But I just want to go on grumbling—see?

MRS. REED. Well, you're not the only one. An' anyhow Ma Peck ought to go—she's got nothin' to live for——

MA PECK (*almost screaming*). I've more than you ever 'ad—yer miserable selfish basket——!

STRANGER (*with sudden authority, taking a pace down to the bar*). Quiet!

(*There is a sudden complete silence. They look at him.*)

I'm disappointed in you. And if I'd known this would lead to such an undignified wrangling scene, I'd have chosen some other method. I thought it would be easy for one of you to volunteer.

STONE (*sullenly*). I don't see what put that silly idea into your 'ead.

MRS. REED. Neither do I.

STRANGER. I think you're forgetting, aren't you? All right then. (*He regards them gravely and with authority, and then makes a great anti-clockwise movement with one hand. This should be accompanied by a ratchety sound, as of a gigantic watch being wound.*)

HARRY. What are you doing?

STRANGER. Putting the clock back. Now then, listen to yourselves.

(*The scene that follows is played exactly as before except that the actors suggest a certain hypnotized effect.*)

HARRY (*as before*). . . . And may we all live a hundred years.

STONE. What for?

HARRY. How do you mean—what for?

STONE. I mean—why do you want to live a hundred years.

HARRY. Oh—I see. Just a saying, that's all. Still, it 'ud be all right to me. To enjoy life, y'know——

MA PECK. Don't talk to this lot about enjoying life. They wouldn't know what you mean.

MRS. REED. Well, just before he came in, you were carrying on—as if you wished you was dead.

MA PECK. Well, so I did, and so would you in my place. As for you, you're dead already, only you don't know it.

HARRY. Now, Ma. Mrs. Reed's all right in her own way, and we're all friends here. I must tell you, I had a good laugh today——

STONE (*cutting in, almost angrily*). Just a minute, Harry Tully. Before you start on the good laugh, I want you to answer just one question for my benefit.

HARRY (*cheerfully*). Go on, I'll buy it.

STONE. What have *you* got to be so cheerful about?

HARRY. Well, what have you got to be so miserable about?

STONE. Do you want me to tell you?

HARRY. No, I've heard it before.

STONE (*almost angry again*). You're no better off than the rest of us. You're in the same old mess-up we're all in. If you're doing as well as I'm doing, I'd be surprised——

HARRY. So would I.

STONE. Well, what's the idea then?

PERCY. If you ask me—and I read a piece about it in a magazine—it's something to do with glands——

IVY (*shocked*). Percy, don't be rude.

PERCY. It's not rude—it's scientific. Glands.

HARRY. Can't say. I don't read magazines. But what I say is this—we're alive and kicking, aren't we? All right then.

PERCY. Yes, but where does that get you?

STONE. Nowhere. He doesn't know what he's talking about.

STRANGER (*laying his fingers on the counter and leaning forward slightly*). Excuse me! And then that's where I came in. Well, you heard yourselves. (*He looks at them gravely, then looks at his watch.*) I can give you five more minutes. After that, if you can't settle who's to go, then it'll be my choice. (*He quietly withdraws one pace from the bar.*)

IVY (*bravely*). He's right. We're all in it but him—Mr. Tully. That's how we talked. As if it didn't matter if we were all dead. (*She hesitates a moment, then looks anxiously at the* STRANGER.) Could it be two—instead of just one? I mean, if it was Percy an' me together, I wouldn't mind so much——

PERCY (*indignantly*). Now just a minute, Ivy. What d'yer want to go pushing us forward for?

STRANGER (*facing* MRS. REED *and the* RANDLES). It can't be two. Only one.

MRS. REED (*frightened*). Don't look at me like that.

HARRY (*to the* STRANGER). All right. Don't let's have any more argument.

(*The* STRANGER *turns slowly to* HARRY.)

Ivy (*astonished*). D'you mean *you're* offering to go——?

Harry (*easily*). Yes. Why not?

Ivy. But you're just the one——

Harry. I know, but what of it? I've enjoyed my life—and we've all to die sometime——

Ivy (*protesting*). It isn't right——

Percy. Shut up, Ivy.

Ivy (*sturdily*). I won't shut up. I say—it just isn't *right* that he should be the one. No, Percy— I'll feel *ashamed* all my life——

Harry (*smiling at her*). Now don't start that, Ivy. Just cheer up—and make him a bit more cheerful too. And look at *him* now.

(*They look, and the* Stranger *is smiling cheerfully*.)

He's got what he wanted, and I believe he knew it was going to be me all the time.

Ivy. Did you?

Stranger (*coming down to the bar*). Just a moment. (*He produces from his inside pocket a small white hand-telephone, and proceeds to talk into it.*) Yes, sir. Number Two District North-East London here. All set, sir. Yes, sir, that's right. Harry Tully. (*He puts away the telephone, withdraws a pace, and smiles at* Ivy *and* Harry.) Yes, I'd a good idea who it would be. If you're frightened of Life, you don't live properly and then you don't like Life. But that doesn't mean you want to die. You're still more frightened of Death. So I guessed Harry, who'd enjoyed life, would be just the one who'd be ready to go.

Ivy. And I still say—it isn't *right* and I feel ashamed—and if it wasn't for 'aving to look after Percy——

Harry. Just forget it, Ivy. And you'll make a man of him yet. (*He looks round at them.*) Well, Mr. Stone, Mrs. Reed, better not let our friend overhear you next time——

(MRS. REED *withdraws a pace from the bar.*)

STONE. You don't catch me coming 'ere ever again.

STRANGER (*grimly*). You would be surprised the places I get into, though.

HARRY. And Ma—look after yourself——

MA PECK (*muttering*). God bless yer—Harry. Always said you was a good lad——

HARRY. Percy, look after the wife here. You're lucky. She's worth ten of you——

IVY (*shyly*). I'm not. But—thank you—for saying it to him. And I'll never forget you—never—never——

(*She crosses to him and kisses him quickly and lightly, then turns back crying, quietly resting against PERCY'S shoulder. He puts a protective arm round her, looking at the others rather defiantly.*)

HARRY. That's the way, boy. Keep on like that. (*He looks at the STRANGER.*) Well, I suppose we're all set for the big jump. Good-bye—the old " Rose and Crown."

STRANGER (*gravely*). And if Life is a rose, then Death is a crown. (*He lifts his voice, looking towards the* L. *corner where the entrance to the other bar is presumed to be.*) All right, sir.

They all stare towards that corner, and then all but HARRY, *who remains at the bar—and of course the* STRANGER *who is farther up stage—draw back looking frightened. The light from the front should now be stronger and direct on* HARRY, *who looks frightened too, watching something, somebody, come in. But then he stops looking frightened, and slowly smiles as if this were an old friend. Then he nods slowly, with the others behind him still looking terrified and awestruck, and the* STRANGER *nodding and smiling, as—*

The CURTAIN *slowly descends.*

FURNITURE AND PROPERTY PLOT

Stage cloth.

ON THE WALLS (*if an ordinary set is used*):
  Advertisements of beers, whiskies, cigarettes, etc.

Bar counter. (*As described in script and on ground plan.*)

(NOTE: *The bar counter should be dead black on the down-
    stage side. On the upstage side, a concealed shelf
    below the counter top.*)

PROPERTIES (*on the concealed shelf*):

  R.C. (*for* STONE). Pint glass of brown ale.
  C. (*for* MRS. REED). Glass of stout.
  L.C. (*for* PERCY *and* IVY). Half-pint glass of bitter beer.
                Half-pint glass of mild ale.
  R.C. (*for* MA PECK). Half-pint glass of brown ale.
  C. (*for* HARRY. *Set to* R. *of* MRS. REED'S *glass*).
                Pint glass of mild and bitter.
                Half-pint glass of brown ale.
                Small glass of port.

PERSONAL PROPERTIES:

  STONE. Pipe. Matches. Newspaper.
  MRS. REED. Shabby handbag.
  PERCY. Cigarettes and matches.
  IVY. Smart but cheap handbag.
  HARRY. Cigarettes and matches.
  STRANGER. Wallet containing several black-edged cards.
                Watch and chain.
                Miniature telephone (white) in inside pocket.
  EFFECT (*off stage*). Loud ratchet. (*See script.*)

GROUND PLAN

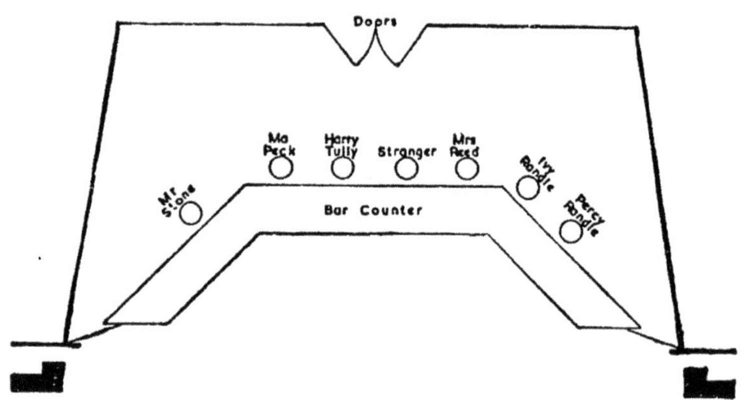

LIGHTING

Floats, NIL.

No. 1 batten: (only) Amber, pink, blue, at $\frac{1}{2}$. Other battens, NIL.

F.O.H. (set P.S.) or P.S. perch: No. 52 gold (frost).

(This spot directs a pool of light on the c. section of the bar. It is at its minimum throughout the play until the cue at the end. Then it fades in, and the batten fades out to NIL as the curtain falls.)

No light on exterior backing; or, amber and blue at $\frac{1}{8}$.

www.ingramcontent.com/pod-product-compliance
Ingram Content Group UK Ltd.
Pitfield, Milton Keynes, MK11 3LW, UK
UKHW021820150726
7214IPUK00017B/229